THE WEATHER
THAT KILLS

THE WEATHER THAT KILLS

POEMS BY PATRICIA SPEARS JONES

COFFEE HOUSE PRESS ≝ MINNEAPOLIS

Cover art: *Going Home,* by Willie Birch

Back cover photograph by Gene Bagnato

Coffee House Press is supported in part by private donations and by grants from: Dayton Hudson Foundation on behalf of Dayton's and Target stores; Bush Foundation; Beverly J. and John A. Rollwagen Fund of The Minneapolis Foundation; General Mills Foundation; Jerome Foundation; National Endowment for the Arts, a federal agency; Lannan Foundation; Star Tribune/Cowles Media Company; The Andrew W. Mellon Foundation; and The McKnight Foundation. This activity is made possible in part by a grant provided by the Minnesota State Arts Board, through an appropriation by the Minnesota State Legislature.

Coffee House Press books are available to the trade through our primary distributor, Consortium Book Sales & Distribution, 1045 Westgate Drive, Saint Paul, MN 55114. Our books are also available through all major library distributors and jobbers, and through most small press distributors, including Bookpeople, Inland, and Small Press Distribution. For personal orders, catalogs, or other information, write to:

Coffee House Press
27 North Fourth Street, Suite 400, Minneapolis, MN 55401

Library of Congress CIP Data
Jones, Patricia Spears, 1955-
    The Weather That Kills / Patricia Spears Jones.
       p. cm.
    ISBN 1-56689-029-2:
    1. Afro-American women—New York (N.Y.)—Poetry. 2. City and town life—New York (N.Y.)—Poetry. 3. Afro-American families—Poetry. 4. Afro-Americans—Poetry. I. Title.
PS3569.P417W43   1995
811'/54—dc20   94-45775
                                                        CIP

10   9   8   7   6   5   4   3   2   1

Special thanks to the late Ray Hill, professor extraordinaire, who understood that I wanted a world away from the mid-South. To Thulani Davis, who sent my poems out into the world when I had almost given up. And to Willie Birch for his art and for watching out for me.

The author also wishes to thank the New York Foundation for the Arts for a fellowship in poetry; the National Endowment for the Arts for a fellowship in poetry; the Squaw Valley Community of Writers for a beautiful place to write and share work; Pamela Painter, David Rivard, Mark Doty, and the wonderful, late Lynda Hull, who made getting an MFA at Vermont College such a pleasure; and to Ruth Maleczech and Lee Breuer of Mabou Mines for their intellectual commitment and artistic fearlessness. To my colleagues at The New Museum of Contemporary Art for their patience and support.

For their dedication, friendship, and help, thanks to Maureen Owen, Jessica Hagedorn, Charles Bernstein, Charlotte Carter, Kimiko Hahn, Bill Allen, Dale Worsley, Wesley Brown, Barry Singer, Elizabeth Murray and Bob Holman, David Carter, Cyrus Cassells, Lorenzo Thomas, Lynn Cadwalder, Paula Elliott, Klare Shaw (the Boston gals), my brother William C. Spears and my sister Gwendolyn Fay Jones.

Patricia Spears Jones

3/11/95

We hanged our harps upon the willows
in the midst thereof.
For there they that had carried us away
captive required of us a song; and they
that wasted us required of us mirth, saying,
Sing us one of the songs of Zion.
How shall we sing the LORD's song in
a strange land?

—*Psalm 137:2—4*
The Holy Bible, King James Version

Come on in my kitchen,
cause it's raining outdoors.

—Robert Johnson
"Come On In My Kitchen Blues"

CONTENTS

The Birth of Rhythm and Blues

FROM THE BILLIE HOLIDAY CHRONICLES

Mid-February in America. Cold everywhere but Florida,
parts of California, and New Orleans, where Mardi Gras ends
in a gale of coconuts, trinkets, streamers and libations.

My daddy came back from the war, tall, slender, handsome.
Lonely in Korea, lonely in Arkansas. Lonely enough
to court my mother. Tall, pretty and tired
of her drunken husband, their store going bankrupt
and the grimy reality of small town daily life. A small town is
gossip and errands, work and more work. Schools closed in
    spring
(chopping cotton) and early fall (picking cotton),
the death-defying lives of all Black people—high yaller to
    coal black.
A Black woman's life is like double jeopardy.
All you win are dreams for your children
and the right amount of lies to make waking worthwhile.
Call it sweet talk from a colored soldier back from the snows
    of Korea.
Back from the nasty jokes, the threats, the fights in This Man's
    Army.
Back to America. Still alive.

Mama is early in her thirties. Promised so little and then
    hungry
for the world. For a world larger than the screen door that
    slams

early morning, and the reeking breath of a man once
    handsome and friendly
and too easy with money. His money. Her time. He's
    beginning to die.
Liver rotting away. He passes blood and thinks of a knife fight,
some juke joint when a Louis Jordan song blasted off the
    jukebox. So fast, that song.
And funny too. Everybody shaking. Pelvic shaking.
But then a man's mouth opened, then another, and then
    slash—high
cheekbones and graveyard eyes. Some niggers don't know
    when to shut up.
A red lightbulb shivers like sunset before a harvest moon.
My mother's husband singes the pain with whiskey. It burns
    the lining of his stomach. Starts the ulcer. Precipitates the
    cancer.
My mother's stomach grows and grows.
New moon. New hope.

My mother sings her own songs. Humming songs.
Something low into the earth
where the hurting stops and healing begins.
That point where Billie hit
bottom and found the start of a global nightmare.
Every walking man wounded again and again. Pierced in eye,
    belly, tongue, penis, anus, shoulder, foot.
All the walking men bleeding and bleeding into
music's deep well. Quenching her joy. Clotting her
dreams. Following her swaying hips screaming GIMME GIMME
    GIMME

Billie's at the corner where the dope man slinks. Willow in a
    Harlem breeze.
She's strung out again. Big Irish cops, with nothing
    better to do, follow her.
She's feeling evil. Starts her humming. They want
    to drink my Irish blood.
They want that back. She's laughing low.

In New Orleans Professor Longhair has taken to the piano
and rumbled up a rhythm as steady as Saturday night loving.
And up North somewhere, someone is dreaming the Fender
    bass.
While across Texas, Black men in shiny tuxedos,
cotton shirts sticking to their skinny torsos,
rise and fall to the beat, the backbeat. A faster shuffle.
A wilder vamp. The beboppers are intellectual, you know,
and fast too. And everyone gets into the aviary act.
Flamingos, Orioles, rocking. Just waiting, just waiting to grind
    you home.

Was it the teasing power of Big Boy Crudup or Ruth Brown's
haughty insinuations or the crazy men in Macon with their
    too tight
suit pants and dicks as long as legend permits,
was it Aretha in the womb listening to Mahalia crooning
and Otis tossing footballs as the marching bands practiced
across the wide fields of the fifties South? Was it ever
so easy to make a voice that seduced and soothed as much as
    Etta James's,
who was pretty as Billie, and soon strung out too.

What made these people, Southern mostly, Black absolutely,
churn up rhythms rich as currents in the Atlantic?

Was it Billie standing in that pool of ugly light?
Fair skin wrinkling. Desperate for the ease of a needle.
Was it ever as sad as this? Not even the grave yet.
Eight more years before the coffin's fit to surround her.
And the men like hellcats cursing the click of her expensive
    heels.
Soft stone in her pocket. Rhinestones in her earlobes.
The dope man's leash shorter and shorter each time the world
    begged for more.

Billie shivers in her skin going slack. Joking the dope down.
Her face maps a bitter terrain.
From pain and back again.
While each door that opens for her, closes.
But now, this moment, the door opens, a crack
where the light bleeds in, stays on her, merciless.

On the lonely roads in Arkansas, Mississippi, Tennessee
and Texas, skinny men in too tight pants shook out the blues.
And up in Chicago, someone with a harmonica wailed and
    wailed
I WANT YOU I WANT YOU I WANT YOU

and out of all the stars that fell on Alabama, Little Richard
    flipped
out of his melodrama and made this scream. His pomaded hair
flinging greasy love to the adoring girls giggling in the
    background.

While the men fingered each one of them.
Was it the first rape or the last smooth flight?

Wailing like the caped saxophone players and the gutbucket
    guitarists,
like the women with *Big* in front of their names—Mama,
    Maybelle—
relentless. Somewhere before the spotlight lengthened
to include so many, so beautiful, so always
rocking rocking rocking till the break of dawn.

Was it ever easy this motion of blood and mucus and dream?
First born and angry at the given world.
A noble operation for Caesar used for a poor Black woman
already wanting to break this wall, as hand claps break a
    forest's
silence. Uterine wall collapsing,
so they cut my mother's belly and drag me out
wailing too.

Officially Lent

Officially Lent and all I want is red meat and wine.
The winter weather cauls this morning,
temperature drops
as fast as Nicaragua's GNP,
while two more Black boys die.

I'd like to believe that all will be for the best.
And yet, what I feel is foolish,
and I did not make this world. So

What? Miles Davis cocked his wry note
on the cusp of the sixties, all sharkskin suit,
fat Italian shades:

the blacker the better.
Struck in the blue smoke haze,
prophet for no one.
Who wants this shit?
And it is, everywhere you step.

Voices—suave, concerned, well paid for—
intone a brief, sad story. Black children, like refugees,
look straight into the expensive lens of the television
    technician,
tell their tales, then return to the task at hand—survival.
Names of friends, classmates, brothers, sisters, cousins
are now carved on a plaque and honorably placed

in the local skating rink—safe house, noisy harbor—where
they try to remember, play.

Botched music
and a violent cycle begins anew.
Blood at the bus stop. Blood in the kitchen. Blood
on the emergency room door.

The weather does not stop this killing.
Not even the last ugly frost which kills the first
foolish narcissus. Wounds as great as these
cannot be stanched. Not before Easter.
They bleed and bleed without healing.
And these children skate and skate.
And we good citizens fan away from the scratch and maul
of their young lives, afraid of the young bloods
cruising the boulevards, radio/tape players
exploding rhythms and base rhymes.
Their only crime is the specter of revenge.
The payback for 400 years of relentless danger.

So what. This woman is hungry. Crackheads are clinging
to some spastic paradise where dreams become destiny.
And it is shit.

The wind's uneven teeth saw against skin.
Cop cars swiftly pass this ambulatory woman on her way
to buy a newspaper. A walk that could get me killed.
I pull my coat tighter. Walk a little faster.
Remember Christmas 1988, my young cousin murdered

by hoods partying too loudly. Murder for requesting a little
    quiet,
a little peace. Christmas Sunday, my mother
kneels at the altar praying for his soul.
For the souls of all young Black men:
shot, stabbed, beaten by each other,
for something as simple as noise. Something
as ordinary as this cold morning wind.

In My Father's House

There was little conversation and too much
store-bought food. Across the dull green carpet,
my father and I tried to make a language
as common to us as our names:
my brief life suddenly more complex.

In my father's house, the rooms stood isolate,
quiet, windows draped heavily like rooms
in the funeral director's mansion—largest
Black-owned home in our little city—
perfumed by furniture wax and Pine Sol.
The kitchen spread out gleaming,
its fixtures shiny, bright as advertisements
in *Good Housekeeping* or *McCall's*.
It seemed so white.

Too neat. No giddy arrangement of toys,
magazines, clothes in need of mending.
The furniture stood stuffed, tufted,
newly bought, carefully placed like the stacks
of bills on his highly polished desk.
Always paid *on time*.

For years, my father stored provisions:
milk, eggs, luncheon meat, Taystee Bread.
He took real meals in "colored" cafes,
roadside joints, where hot-sauced pork chops,
mushy collard greens and mashed potatoes thickened

his waist, knotted his heart. Stomach-
ache, heartache washed away with aspirin
and Johnnie Walker Red.

His big Chevy rolled over St. Francis, Lee and
Crittenden counties from his downtown barbershop
to his well-kept rent houses. There were occasional visits
with lady friends scattered across the Delta.
Matrimony-minded widows, spinsterish school teachers,
even a deaconess.

My father's voice boomed toward me.
A drum in the belly fierce little eyes
that stared down at me. Dreaming. Day
dreaming, while he stirred the Campbell's soup.
I'd spin his jazz and pop albums.
Portraits of the great "colored" stars:
Brook Benton, Dinah Washington, Johnny Mathis
adorned the hi-fi record covers: bits of confetti
left at the party the host was too tired to clean up after.

I'd listen to the albums' bright music
wishing the swirling strings, their incessant backbeat,
would make me love my father.

But who is father? First memory:
my mother's first husband dead before my fourth birthday.
Now, this big, brown-skinned, sad-eyed man so full of charity,
so great with solicitude, humbled by his desire for "daughter."

He stutters encouragement as I give a report
listing my weekly achievements, our
Sunday meal completed.
I wait for twilight's too slow descent,
when I'll enter the big Chevy;
then cross the divide between
my father's house,
my mother's home.

Taking the Curve

(A COUNTRY SONG)

The faster you go
the smoother the turn
when you slow down
there are too many choices.
The light turns red.
You get rear-ended.
Sideswiped, cursed and dejected.
What you want is the smooth highway
and a long journey to a beautiful place

And when you get there
you will hear the sweet rough voice
of a woman from Arkansas.

Singing about her man,
her blessed life,
her heart so full of joy
and all the comforts of home.

In Like Paradise/Out Like the Blues

I.

huddled over his acoustic guitar, he heard
voices from the center of the earth
(sonorous revolutions per minute transmitting)
MUTANT
MUTANT
You've fooled around too long.

2.

After Rufino Tamayo returned from mapping
the Cosmos, he turned to his wife and said

Stars are like flowers in the desert.
They shiver fresh in the aeon knowing
that they will become memory, hunger,
the core of dreams.

It is up to me, then, to bring back their beauty:
taut, seamless before the eyes of men and women.
To amplify the vitality of their illumination
(righteous shimmer above melancholy clouds)
To remind humanity that without them
night would never come.

3.

The death of a star like the death of a flower
is awesome, ugly, a relentless warning.

4.

Artists make whole somehow the ways
in which dreams persist.
Each of us turns to the hunger of stars
and wipes the crumbs from our mouths.

On canvas, they laugh like children.
In essence, they scream like children. And struggle
like children to eat, grow, copulate, then flash out.
A name perhaps. A body gone.

5.

Heeding the wails of heaven—frenzy
of hard-loved electric guitars—he removed
the soft strings from his life, one by one.
He replaced each of them with fool's silver.
Steel. Blueheated. Oxidized.
Glistening. Sweat like gold rivers flowing
down the face of a man black as the hunger of stars.

His urgent guitar flaming
His body hungry hungry hungry
Cocaine/methedrine
Slim women hovering about him, specters.
Thirsty. He is weeping.
Some *thing* got lost.
A man who plays fire never stays to dinner.
Is welcome in the house of the living only so long.
And then there are the photographs, the videos.
Gossip. Memorabilia.

Songs on the radio at tender hours—five past
midnight or three A.M.

The death of one so young is angry. Ugly.
A sin perhaps. Dust. Secrets. Forever. Gone.

6.
You've got to know when you're weary
So you will lie down and rest.

You've got to know when you're weary
So you'll lie down and rest.

If you take your dreams serious
You may get yourself blessed.

7.
Like legacy. Like Paradise.
Like the crushed perfume of a captive flower.
Like the notation of your very first breath
Like memory

Like the cradle rocking in the heart of a poet
back and forth
back and forth

you've got to know when you're weary
so you will lie down and rest.

What You Know

It is not the memory I can conjure,
daily destruction, daily dope,
Saigon in spring. In summer, heat too much.

What you give are your poems,
each a piece of the stone
that was your heart.

I have no way of finding
that point of pain,
crystalline as methedrine,
steady as tropical rain.

There are prayers, say some, strong enough
to shake blood from your hands,
death from your eyes.

You do what you can and, sometimes,
you make music

as volcanic as a boy's laughing fit.
Your walk is the walk of a man in need of gravity,
you smile. And back of your talk is the blues,

ancient, bold. Hellhounds on your tail?
Each one snarls a signature note from the man in Mississippi

who knew what you know, who could see straight
through the thick tobacco smoke, the club's
hard red-light glow,
to the lit-up forehead of a woman waiting to love.

Encounter and Farewell

It's all foreplay, really—this walk
through the French Quarter exploring souvenir shops,
each of them carefully deranged, as if dust were to settle
only at perfect intervals. Yes to the vetiver fan
that smells sweeter than sandalwood or cedar.
No to the mammy doll dinner bells.
No to the mammy dolls whose sewn smiles are as fixed
as the lives of too many poor Black women here:
motherhood at twelve, drugged, abandoned by fifteen,
dead by twenty (suicide, murder) so easily in Desire.
And yet, their voices sweeten the snaking air,
providing the transvestites their proper Muses,
all of whom have streets named for them in the Garden
    District.

A soft heat settles on Terpsichore,
just inside the gay bar where the owner's pink flamingos
complement silly songs on the rescued Rockola.
Who can dance to that Lorne Greene ballad, "Ringo"?

Dixie beer is the beer of choice; marijuana the cheapest
drug. Relaxation is key, since it's all a matter of waiting
for the right body to stumble toward you. Lust perfumes
parties in the projects, barstool chatter at the Hyatt,
lazy kissing on the median strip stretching down
    Tchoupitoulas.
If Professor Longhair were alive, he'd teach a lesson

in perfect motion: the perfect slide of a man's hand
down a woman's back;

a lesson you learned long ago before you met me. We are
making love as we did before in Austin and Manhattan.
But in this room on this costly bed our lovemaking
starts out the slowest grind, then, like this city's weather,
goes from hot to hotter, from moist to rainstorm wet.

You're tall, A., and where there should be tribal markings
there are scars—football, basketball, mid-sixties grind parties
where something always got out of hand. There's the perfect
amen. You're your own gospel.
And you bring good news to me—the way you enter me
like grace, the way you say my name, a psalm.
No. That's not it. It's the engineer in you that
gets me. Your search for the secret line that goes
straight to the center of the earth. Deeper and deeper
you go until there's no earth left in me. And we
hum and moan a song as old as our selves gone back.

There are too many souvenirs in your eyes.
Gifts given too often, too hastily, never opened.

Outside a city sprawls its heat, seeks out every pore,
licks every moment of sweat as we shiver in this chilly room
taking each other's measure. We say good-bye again and again.
As if every kiss, every touch we make will shadow
all our celebrations.

And they do.

If I Were Rita Hayworth

I would hear Spanish first.
My father would teach me how to shimmer.
My mother would keep her mouth shut.

I would wear red dresses at age 12
and dance like a woman many years older.
I would dance in my father's arms.

Later I would dye my hair red
and pluck the last Spanish words from my mouth.

I would masquerade as an American—
that healthy girl next door who knows
how to crack a whip.

I would dream only in black and white
(after Technicolor, some peace is needed).

As the Studio built a whole world for me
full of fresh cream and gingerbread, I would seek
out the darkest men, nigger dark, then fuck them
into marriage. I would wed a Prince of Darkness
and bear daughters named for the perfumes of Arabia.

If I were Rita Hayworth, strung between living a lie
and bearing a sickness so furious it ages me to dream of it,
I would rage in my illness, make a black hole
wide enough to swallow the damnation of my beauty.

The Usual Suspect

FROM THE BILLIE HOLIDAY CHRONICLES

Satin gown the color of black
sand under full moonlight.
Voice colored jewel rich. Ruby rouge. Cat's-eye
green. Blue at autumn twilight blue.
She's got this big sad heart.
When she sings, she sings the world's real dream:
love, faith, money.
The world's real problem: love, fear, death.

She's gorgeous. Full storm. NO WARNING
Her voice sweeps couples together.
It is that *real weather*
that kills and kills
and makes the day so new.

She tells a thousand stories—no, one thousand and one.
A Scheherazade night after night, conjuring her dreams.
So the torchlights flame in the street
and blood rushes pell-mell from heart to lung to feet.
Every bent note spins like a ballroom's gaudy globe
on an axis of hope: that tomorrow the fly figure
of a pomaded man will make the troubles glow away.
Life, as always, is too real now—
battles over there; the lynch-throated barefoot man, here.
Flag-draped coffins traveling to segregated cemeteries
while colored troops guarding German POWs beg to hear Lena
    Horne.

It's a gambler's moon, the troop trains' keen departures.
So elegant this grand weeping beneath vaulted ceilings
in cities with Indian names, where old men sell whatever
takes away the worry: massively floral perfumes,
cheap Havanas and cheaper reefer, and the latest recordings
of a woman fragrant with gardenia blossoms,
tobacco and Florida water. There are times when only the
    spring
in her throat offers the essential prayers.
And even then, the world trips, stumbles and falls away
from her voice as if deaf, dumb and blind.

Remember Iwo Jima

FROM THE BILLIE HOLIDAY CHRONICLES

Every time I play "Them There Eyes"
I sing along, trailing a half-beat behind,
as if holding the notes can bring my wife back.
I got too much gin in me. Start up loud.
Remembering the girl I met, married.
The woman I lost. And Billie's voice
outlines my desire. A wet wind off a mighty storm.

The record spins, a relic. Like this drink.
And the weather feels like the end of winter,
full of promise. Not fair.
When I met her she was this cute blonde. Curvy.
At the USO. One of the nice girls. Nice to me.

I never liked the "songbirds," those slim blondes
with high snappy voices. They could be sweet.
But I was city-bred and full of blues.
Shiny shoes on Saturday night.
Before Uncle Sam sent me the letter that sent me to hell.
Billie could go there. To hell, and come back
laughing about it.
So when I fell for her, I took her to see Billie.
Wanted to find the edges to her curves, see if she
could trace the fear rising within me.
Would she know what Billie knew?

I was a fool. She danced as if she had no spine.
Spinning out the cracks between beats like the colored girls
at the Savoy, though not as fast. Once I said to her,
You must have some nigger blood in you.
She laughed as if it didn't mean a thing.

The Blues of This Day

for Miles Davis

The blues of this day
are as elegant and as sad
as minor thirds and we all try to sing it.

What we want is to be brass.
The horn-scratched voice blown through.
Valves as golden as his. Lord as crazy sex
or first real heartbreak.

It was always his back slightly bent away
from all of us who adored him, gazing across his

shoulders as the band jumped into the party
one solo at a time.
Or they could be rocking way off-key
going as far away from the melody as Venus to Mars.
Funk can be as easy as that
getting together in the dark.

And as hard as the breaking light
that catches the throat of sated lovers, the morning after.
The talk the night before by the last of hip men
who knew the way of the world and then some,
about Miles and his two steps ahead of the century
like the first Black man to leave the Delta humming

I gotta go, but I can't take you.
I gotta go, but I can't take you.
If you want to follow, then do what you want to do.

Wheel of Fortune

Every turn is unfair. Someone knows the score,
but is sworn to secrecy.
If you give the wrong answer, you get nothing.

But if you're lucky and the pointer hits: YES
You get dinner, money, a new sedan, the keys to that beach
    house
in the Hamptons.

It's like Poetry. Out of a bowl of Chaos, you fish
for the perfect question. If it is lucent,
the audience cheers, then calculates prizes. (Often meager,
they nonetheless arise from being lucky.)

And good luck tastes better than cornstarch,
cheap coffee and stale beer.

But if the audience discovers a mistake,
will they forgive the poet's claim of inspiration?

She takes the last stanza and spins it,
but it keeps going out of control.

At last, the game show blonde, her brunette co-host
and the fellow contestants weary of waiting
for the poet's ultimate trope. They give up.
Turn off the lights. Go home.

In the enveloping solitude, she dares to speak.
From her mouth a flock of blackbirds.
In flight her voice streaks the spark
wings make on the sharp edge of lunar light.

Joss Sticks

in memory of Frances Chung

The coffin appears to hold two Frances Chungs:
Frances, dutiful daughter, teacher.
Frances, poet, mythmaker, chronicler of
farces.

Facing this coffin—so large
it could contain another body—her family sits.

Huge wheels of flowers greet each of us mourners.
Red flowers, pink ones, orange too
as white satin streamers slash the bouquets
with Chinese ideographs:

Do they say, "Good-bye, you've been good"?
Do they say, "Life is too short and pain too long"?
Do they say, "Forgive her"?

I feel like a fraud here. I don't know Chinese. I don't know
the rite in this grieving. I do understand her mother who
rises up weeping, then falls back into her chair. Her son
    catches
her, gentle.

People walk in, bow toward the family, then walk
to the middle of the room, where a large urn holds
hundreds of joss sticks. Each picks a new one, lights it
then adds the lit stick to all the others.

As incense rises to the electric light,
they bow before the coffin, then return to their seats.

I sit on the side, watch. The incense is as constant
as noisy Mulberry Street traffic. In the only
playground in Chinatown, children are squealing, cursing,
while the winter heat dissipates.

Before leaving, I pick up a piece of folded white paper.
And hard candy. Inside the paper is a nickel. Prosperity.

The hard candy is pure sugar. Sweetness. Soon it is all gone.
Like this life spent so quickly, and yes, we are sweeter for it.
Mulberry Street's nasty bustle stops my tears.

Frances would have found the proper, nuanced emotion
in the elaborate scenes in Chinese opera. How the young
    maiden
finds her way across the mad river, yet dies before her true love
can claim her. Or how a young woman moves from China to
    Guatemala
to the rumble of New York's Chinatown with a face forever
    young.
She would have made a tender, witty poem
like one in *Ordinary Women*
that we printed on the eve of a new decade.
When the first sweetness tasted best.

San Francisco, Spring 1986

I feel so East Coast. Shut down, frantic.
Too used to the expensive, the hot-house flowers sold on
every corner. Here the flowers brighten every corner. Free.
Here, the wildflowers are different. Calla lilies grow wild?
Silky, white, trumpet, shaped, composed,

As is this midday light.
Translucent in the Embarcadero.
White, hot, harsh in the Mission.
There, the pink, gray and yellow stucco houses
shutter themselves against the brutal splendor.

As I and Roberto sip beer and talk poetry, politics, the growing
    list
of men with AIDS, heat is almost forgotten in the midday
    darkness
of this Salvadoran restaurant.
We patrons linger over plates of rice and beans, vivid spices
harry our hunger as the beers splash down our throats.

This cool seems dreamlike.
Our meal timeless.
But time does matter.

Men here, lovers, friends, are
learning women's work.
The weary labor of mothers, sisters, aunts.

How many pills?
Can we afford this?
Here's the doctor's private number.
All the statements that pave the way
for rest, guilt and more work
with someone else.

Here's where the caring begins. Here's where
the caring works. Even as lovers defiantly declare,

"I know he's dying. I won't get tested.
Not just yet."

Here's where the time is taken.
Here's where the story matters.
Where the weeping and the anger
commence.

As if the hard-bodied men
so very young in the Castro,
enterprising in the Haight,
discreet in the Mission
compose an army fighting blind.

And who could be blind to this city's beauty?
Where century-old eucalyptus rend
cathedrals before stone and the sun's lush glow
halos the rise and fall of exhausted hills.

What is so easily available here—the green coast
and an ocean at war with its name—is not so easily
taken away.
These men dying are not given up without love,
without caring, without a fight.

Christmas, Boston, 1989

This is how I know God exists:
God made cold.

God made sky the color of milk
God lets children eat their breath.

At the corner of the plaza, women in expensive coats
praise God's name. JESUS, they shout.

Jesus slaps back.
Wind on cheek. Every tremble a sign.

At twilight, his most faithful servants
present oblations: wine bottles, beer cans,

half-eaten donuts, orange rinds, banana skins,
cups and cups of black sugarless coffee.

Couples dance across icy streets, glad
to get from one side to the other.

Left behind are winter gifts:
gloves, socks, boots, brassieres.

Across the parched milky sky,
electric lights bloom.

Lost Manhattan

As the rich walk carelessly past the blind,
past the lame poor whose cupped hands
and alert stance become sidewalk furniture

as each traffic light signals a sharper
image of speed, then we can

torch the building. Then watch light expand
as the crows return to Tompkins Square.

The city shrouds itself in fog, every track collapsed
like the veins of old junkies as the crackheads dance, so
quick you think planet dance planet dance
planet dance.

Gossip

Charlie Parker died of heartbreak, or everything.
And Marilyn, the love of Kennedys.
Rock Hudson died from a loss of beauty, his own,
face shrunken, softened, no longer mineral hard.

What is this desire to wrap the celebrity dead in paper,
blood, wings and shit. To toss them in the fire and wait
for the ashes to mass, a stinking incense?

Light illumines Marilyn's drained skin.
Rock's kisses are suspect.
And Parker's laughing tempo stops on a dime.

We love to watch them float away.
To heaven.
To hell.
Who really cares?

What we love is the failing, the falling.
It is what we do not speak of
when the radio plays
something memorable
and we lack the skill
to carry the tune.

Baby Hair Shirt

for Chrysanne Stathacos and Paloma Hagedorn Woo

here is a conventional dress pattern
short sleeves, high waist, slightly flaring skirt
if this dress could swing as dresses do in summer
it would swing with the best of them
but this is not a dress

it is made of handmade paper
stained by black tea
veined by human hair

not the infant's fine hair
but thick, heavy strands
that twine through the dress
like veins beneath a baby's skin
exposed, a living highway

this dress form is as stiff
as the one worn by the Infanta
in that portrait by Velázquez

La Infanta, baby princess
stands poised, ladylike, prepared
to assume her considerable privilege
as infant
as royalty
as daughter of the ugliest king in Europe

who sits astride numinous stallions
as the Inquisition strips away the flesh
of the sinful
the intellectual
the Jews and the Moors
whose hair has not the fine, lank texture
of the king's coiffure

but whose ideas have a power even Velázquez recognizes,
secretes in his shadowy portraits of Philip and his family

His harsh brushstrokes comb the pointed beard
of the regent, streak the soft folds of the Infanta's
silk dress, catch the sour breath of a dying empire

as does Chrysanne's miniature dress

that types the wearer (if there was a wearer)
surrounds her in a token of pain

not the first hard thrust into life's bright air
but the daily material that makes a life being lived

choices and consequences pinching the nerve
spirit over flesh
joy or despair
love or the dream of it
pricking the skin, dancing in the veins

mocking the girl's goodness

making the grim details of the baby's growing up
a laughing matter like cancer of the esophagus
or a shotgun blast to the heart

A Question of Weather

"Hot enough for you?" If another raspy-voiced stranger
asks this question of me, I shall throw my dirty sweatshirt
in his face. Just like that. Or throw this cool tropical drink
in the waitress's pretty face.

Of course, it is *hot* enough. The lantana's bright
blossoms radiate a tropical glory beneath a sun
that beams and beams. Oh happy entity.

My God, the last time birds sang like this
I was thirteen. My limbs ached. And every gland
shivered in anticipation.

I want this sour taste on my tongue to leave.
If only my companions could greet the heat
with different words. Words as generous, kindly,
dazzling as the sun.

We humans sweat. We try
to make contact.

But, once the gargantuan lawn mower stops,
the birds utter a conspiracy of voices. A secret
about to be broken.

And every dance I know itches my feet.

Glad All Over

I saw Julian Bond in 1965 at a SNCC rally,
just outside this shack on the side of town where
I was not supposed to be.
It was even poorer than where I lived.
I was curious. Everyone was curious.
This was about *organizing*. But were we ready?
As ready as Black folk in West Memphis, Marianna,
Helena. Up and down the Delta. Was it so bad
that there could be no turning back?

In a mythic retelling, I could say I joined SNCC,
attended every meeting, rallied all my friends,
marched every march.
But mothers have eyes and ears everywhere in small towns
and mine found out.
She wanted change as bad as she wanted the schools
    integrated,
hot running water in our house, a car loan paid off,
and a husband who did more than scream at her daily
before he went to wherever he worked. But first
things first. I, eldest daughter. She, working mother.
No contest. At home I had to watch my brother and sister.
Tend to the house falling down. Some of my classmates
    marched
to the center of the city, were jailed. A boycott began.
It seemed as if it failed, this boycott.
But downtown was dying since Black folk weren't buying.
The Chamber of Commerce refused to say it was so.

It seemed as if nothing changed. For a while, I stood
on the sidelines as those becoming mythic figures of history
crashed by. Until the day Arkansas state troopers stood
in the front of my mother's house, high-powered rifles aimed
at the people on my street—my childhood in gunsight.
This after our neighbors—a father and two sons—were
    arrested
by the corrupt sheriff, taken to jail, then released to the
    waiting

Klan. They got out alive, but only after broken collarbones,
    broken
legs, hemorrhages, bruises, contusions, stomped-on dreams.
I see my mother, who until that day could not say *shit*,
go up to one of the troopers and politely, quietly demand:
"Sir, see these children. Please lower your rifle."
He did.

Later that night, every house in my neighborhood stood ready.
The only lights visible were streetlamps.
My brother and a friend sat on our front porch,
loaded shotguns in their laps. Waiting, waiting for any white
    man
to come down Division Street. Inside our house, my mother
    prayed,
and I started this poem that returns every twelve years
like a labor that must be done
if I am to ever grasp my mother's feat,
our family's ordinary courage.

It's hard to see children in T-shirts that read "Any Means
    Necessary"
and know that they have not sat as my brother
sat on a porch with a rifle waiting, just waiting to kill
any white man fool enough
to be a member of the Klan.

So, yes, we did not all meet the firehoses in Birmingham,
or face down Chicago police in a battle for the hearts and
    minds
of suburbanites fearful that Fred Hampton, George Jackson,
    even
the dead Martin Luther King would disturb their manicured
    lawns.
"Glad all over" bubbles up, the secret joy beneath grim
    turbulence
of a decade now known as much for the pursuit of pleasure as
    for
political assassination, a war broadcast nightly, lawless police,
ritual murder and hard, harsh truths. Getting harder.

The Perfect Lipstick

When the life-sized replicas of the Niña,
the Pinta, and the Santa María
precariously sailed into New York harbor,
they looked like toy ships.

Just think, Columbus in a toy ship.
Off to discover the perfect route—
the fastest way to China, the Indies,
all that spice.

He never got this far north.
But all the same, the slaughter of whole peoples,
buildings that even God had not thought of in 1492,
and "expulsion," "discovery," the "Slave Trade"
all followed.

Out of this horror came
new foods
new clothes
new shoes
a language as mixed as the blood of the people
and as alienating.

But there are times when the connections, no matter how
    fragile,
hold, like the thick sails of those tall ships
which decorated the harbor—July 4 in fog and gentle light.

It is why I appreciate my favorite shade of lipstick:
Sherry Velour.

Sounds like the name of a drag queen from the early seventies.
One of those strapping Black men who had enough of playing
    macho,
put their feet in five-inch heels and made saints of Dinah
    Washington,
Rita Hayworth and a very young Nina Simone.

So, on goes this lipstick. Pretty for parties.
Fatal for festivals.
Sherry Velour and her hot discoveries:
light above the fog,
a toy ship.
Black men in sequined dresses and the click of new words
in the new world where the most dangerous of dreams
come true.

Healing Sheath
for The Clash

So I was in a Heresies meeting when Holly read this letter
    smuggled out
of Greenham Common, detailing the women's militancy and
    the viciousness
of the police. Ungunned, black-booted men in full riot gear
    who could hit a woman, any woman, as easily
as they could extol the virtues of tea or ale.
You could hear a bitter history in our reading this letter out
    loud.
You could hear a world tearing itself.

In the meantime, nuclear arms are landed elsewhere in
    England,
in Germany, in some nice-sounding towns in France.
Payback came, years later, to the Brits. What with the
    European
Community, Thatcher's escape from more than one IRA
    bomb, and the *Pakis* to beat on or the occasional Irish lad
with a bad temper and a knowledge of Marx.

Like the boys out of London, brash and ripping
their wry commentary a splattering rhythm and frantic bad
    guitar.
Their crazy, crazy sadness got up in rock-and-roll guise:
slicked-back dirty hair, T-shirts and torn jeans,
and, yes, as black-booted as their police counterparts outside
    the barbed gates.

An earnest stylishness, perfect rebellion, bad teeth even,
stomping the gallows before morning comes again
to America where they will play mean and hard for a lot of
      money
and lose their dreams at the end of a long night's limousine.

When just like in Dickens the fires dim on winter nights
and the mothers outside Greenham Common curse the
      warriors
and the nuclear warheads ease into berths from England to
      Alaska,
Brixton poor Black and Irish kids drum down police
with sticks, glass, stones who get bloody injury and early death
for their ordinary street dancing.
Someone intones platitudes,
but the beat breaks another back.

Sly and the Family Stone Under the Big Tit

ATLANTA, 1973

We waited and waited. Stoned for Sly. Southern sons and
      daughters
of the Rainbow Tribe. Under Georgia Tech's Big Tit.
Sucking in the marijuana, blowing out the heat.

Former debs with shag cuts and torn jeans their good old boy
friends who used to hunt and fish, now glitter-rocked, ready
with red painted nails and the latest Mott the Hoople tape
on their dashboards. Rebel boys back from 'Nam who used
to party with the brothers on the DMZ—that is, when they
were not beating the shit out of each other before the
VC struck up yet another victorious attack.

Sly's the perfect foil for this crowd.
"Sex Machine" and "Don't Call Me Nigger, Whitey" are
our anthems of choice. "I want to take you higher" just seems
      like
dessert. And of course, Sly is late.
Real late. Sly may not even be in the vicinity.
Like the airport.

Then the house lights actually dim.
The band comes out ragged. Like every musician from
      Provence to Paducah,
they have to play, but their bodies droop. Their songs droop.
And Sly appears indeed to be stoned. By this time the audience
could care less. The show would've gone on. We could sing
      this shit.

We could take the stage and trash it. We could suck beers and colas

till the aluminum disappeared.

This is the end of the mighty rainbow. The brothers in huge Afros,

amulets and attitudes stalk the round of the Big Tit, checking, checking

everybody out. And blond boys with open paisley shirts parade their chest hair

and tight pants like so many peacocks, while we girls

just catch the magnificent promenade.

Between the air outside and the air in here,

there are worlds galore. And we want it all.

The Rainbow Tribe picks up the mess of miscegenation,

our cluttered history, and walks outside.

Into the Georgia night. Fucked up and full of spleen.

Ripped off, someone yells.

But we all had a good time. Really.

Waiting for the California soul sound

to wash over us like an ocean wave,

like something we've dreamed about but

could not hear. Like a song of peace.

Sly Stone under the Big Tit, pretty in that messy-colored California way.

Making music happen while the lights in his eyes dimmed.

And we too wanted to make something work that couldn't.

The sex machine switched off.

The highs were plummeting.
An avalanche of choices awaiting all of us.

But all we wanted was to party. To mess around with the mess
   around.
To shift ourselves out of the Georgia sun-stroked days
and turn into each other's arms as Family,
and loving always loving the way we thought the world
   should be.

5:25 A.M.

for Robert

You're not a saxophone
key of permanent blue
nor the plumed serpent electric guitar
come to breakfast on fire

Into storms that shift invisible
your voice grounds deep
in the wake of something new.
(That's why the light burns in the bathroom.)

The weight of you
is traced on my sheets by musk, semen
oil of coconut (your hair).

An African profile hardened into that dance
the old one where shoulders lean
into cracks between Motown harmonies.
(That's why the stereo's too loud.)

And what you mean, the African American dream:
he was smart
so he walked
as if he
was going somewhere
important.
(That's why the buses are late.)

Around you always this halo of music
a song so sweet, it makes teeth ache.

Falling Magic

When is the flu flu-like
and when is a man a hero?
What do we make of this smile
and, otherwise, this despair?

An athlete's body, solid,
melts; a politician's eye weeps.

The world is a tricky place.
Somewhere between the sheets

a woman comes for more
then falls down again, too tired.

And somewhere else a memory:
man, woman, party, sex.

It's easy to believe in the other guy
and his poison. It's easy to forget that flesh

is sweet and vulnerable. That each one
of us will die. It's easy to forget until

one man's superb body falters.
And even grown men stand before their mirrors

wondering while children joke about it and ponder.
Remember for the moment death's petty whisper.

As if the forgetting stops at the door.
And what enters the mind is the dream of a full life

stopped by the invisible, the accidental, the foolish.

Blumen

Irises cost as much as a cheap breakfast.
They are no longer thirsty, opening, drenched blue,
Saturated blue. The color of English

under a Munich sun. Oh, but in Berlin
flowers shiver. The gray, drizzly day
becomes gray, drizzly night. When the sun blanches
the massive columns on the *Unter der Linden*,
it looks like the punch line to a very odd joke.

The poor are laughing the laughter of the hungry and weary.
And under found umbrellas, everyone searches for what else
may have been left behind.

A photographer is almost starving. Yes, today there was bread,
and two nights before, a sort of meat. He lives a few blocks
    from the statue of Hegel.
That stern, patriarchal bust reminds him of an uncle who
    spoke Latin.
In his domicile, silver nitrate spikes the air.

Across the boulevards, citizens fight citizens. A wrestling match
in the grand manner—vicious, politically controlled and
    magnificently
ugly. And the rest of Europe comes to gawk.
To play. To read the latest report of depravity, cannibalism,
sodomy, the escapades of celebrities—who sleeps with what.

The photographer is heartbroken. These blossoms cost more
    than
thirteen-year-olds selling fake innocence for a sip of
    something sweet.
Seven irises. A fortune in bread and butter. Seven irises in a
    white vase.
The crack in the porcelain turned toward the darkness.
The flowers marked by dusty light.
As if lifted into the floating world. It is not the money, which is
    worthless.
It's the image. Irises floating in the silvery dust.
Irises were her favorite. The woman, no, the child he loved.
Chinese flowers. Japanese. From anywhere east of this rain.
She loved the expensive arrangements, their brilliant color.
She saw *The Blue Angel* and thought she looked sexier
than Dietrich. She thought she could sing. She thought she
    could play the part.
That she could eat whenever she wanted to. Fool.
Seven irises. A perfect architecture.
House with a spiky roof, no windows. Desperate for water.
Dried blood drawn from
her slender throat—cut. Her veins—cut. Her face bashed in.
    Her sex disprized.
Seven irises. Seven sins.

The photographer is crying. He studies the print.
The irises open, then fall into this botched posture
two of them droop over, drunken. Each space between
flower, between leaf and the wall behind is the distance love
    travels

from wish to shattered peace. This print costs everything
he's got: money, heart, ideals.

His hunger keeps him inside, away from the shouts and blows
in the street. Later, he will betray friends, fight in vicious
    battles,
survive to see Berlin in rubble, in shadow and shame.
A half-century will go by.
But, at the moment, his hand holds the print,
a gift for a woman dead to all but him.

And the print survives. A mysterious dust holds the flowers
upright almost, like drunken lovers holding each other up,
somehow. Later, someone finds the negative unblemished,
then makes a new print, crisp and historic.
As expensive as silence.

Silence under a streetlamp as the murderous client
walks away from his crime. Not even a whistle through his
    teeth.

Thief's Song
for Thulani Davis

In this film, Neruda defends a young poet's
theft of his metaphors.

A young woman rolls an egg
across her generous breast.

Everyone speaks Spanish
as the jukebox plays the Beatles' version
of "Please Mr. Postman."

Off camera, President Allende dies
an ugly, dangerous death.

Allende's ideas are tossed about,
so many shells in a relentless storm.

Then the film follows Neruda's sad decline:

his feet upon rocky terrain,
eyes on miraculous water.

Solitude: heart of eternal fire.
Psalm: bridge between dream and sky.

You Just Got the Call

for Keith Haring

Swish, you put on your underwear,
your gold tooth, torn jeans
and the leather chain from Tuesday.

A new day has come up out of the East River
chilly, delicious, full of too many things.

Sleet, rain, fifteen accidents on the L.I.E.
and the fax machine is down at the studio.

You point your black-booted feet toward heaven,
then fall through thin ice. Seven times seven

is older than you. Has more numbers.
Makes as much money as the podium-headed business-
men at Amsterdam and 85th or Second Street and Avenue D.
But this is what you've been waiting for. This

time last year, you were quarreling with the planet.
Sick. Like so many others. Sick and fighting mad.
Numbers. Numbers. Numbers. White cell count. Down.
How many breaths does it take to make a life, living?
How many to end it? Trick question.

The oops of life like a stadium wave
wraps the planet.
Up and down. You street-smart son of Suburbia.

A quick fuck on the turnpike between the smoke
and aw-shucks of another opening.

You just got the call
and there's so much to do.
Make more happy/crazy dramas on the subway advertising
sheets: mama/papa/radiant BABY halo surround in chalk.
Their dog leads them. Comic beast signifying
Trickster America—new angel for the coming millennium.
Thanks for so full a vision given freely
in an era of dangerous greed and too easily satisfied lust.

Payback's a bitch. And the count is way down.
Blood, shit, semen and phlegm smear the blank canvas.
An artist's death. You get three-quarters of a
New York Post, page three. And the headlines too.
We get the beginnings of a *retablo.*
Out of blood comes warning. Out of ambition
the genesis of a fable. Shrines are for burning.
As is the barrel on Houston Street where your mural
remains vandalized by colleagues. Silly, their jealousy,
their anger. The fiery barrel is no eternal flame.
It's a street stove for the homeless men who were there
when you came and who are there now. Trash and fire
wetting their chilled faces.

April

for Gene Bagnato

in the Greenwich Village doorway, two men
kissing, stop, start laughing.

A book jacket's constructivist type,
handsome in bold black, red and white
hawks *The Book of Pain.*

Accidental illiteracy: it is titled
The Book of Rain.

And it costs too much.

Today, it feels harder to care.
Sunshine's a weak promise, as are daffodils
poking up out of the battered soil
in Washington Square.

Later on the Uptown IRT, this legless man
scoots toward each of us, seeking
gifts of spring:
the intemperate flesh of new lovers,
the gauzy music of crisp cotton skirts,
prep-school boys' flawless mirth,
the hard-won indifference of past mugging victims.

We drop not a dime in his dirty palm.
Unsurprised by our obduracy,

he swings out the door onto the subway platform
where a short, fat Russian man plays
"Stars and Stripes Forever" on an amplified harmonica.

Walking up the dingy stairs
at 72nd and Broadway, there is just enough
faith in muddled weather to remember
nature's seasonal sufficiency.

First, those struggling flowers.
Then, as the yellow to green leaves fan
out like new skirts on a windy day,
sweet singing birds come feasting
in the very center of the city.
Followed by bright strokes of lightning
arching the Hudson. Thunder's callous
drumming resonates.
As again, rain falls cold,
but not as cold as the day before.

Bête Noire

Every day another excuse
laundry
shopping
a letter home explaining the need
for repayment of a small loan

Maybe wine will loosen its grip
or a slow fuck with a new man—maybe not.

Got to get out of the clutches
Despair—not hard enough
Depression—not fair

In the fifteenth meeting
where the angels stopped talking
all the bad news gathered to one side of the room
like the fast girls did in high school

THE STORIES I COULD TELL YOU

but this *bête noire*
this creature from another language
has my drama in a hammerlock
and my soul on hold.

What I remember is Ralph Lemon
in a skirt. I wanted it, the skirt.
He was fanning himself and posing the question:

Can a beautiful Black man
become a pretty white woman?

Only in the heart, I answered.
Bête noire laughed only in New York.

Rhythm and Blues Two

An old song becomes a dream of you
as beautiful as one of those vast blue spring days
that only New Yorkers know about.

Here I sit, coffee drunk, wondering what will happen
when my senses cease.
Between my desire for you and your damned departures,
can't sleep enough/ there are too many dreams.

I watch the edge of this internal magic
sharpen as everywhere your face, lips,
hands and groin demand
the final kisses before I throw you out the door.
Before you find someone else,
someone new. Who knows?
If I toss my tears across the pillow
or call my girlfriends and complain
how will I accept the beauty of this pain?

I sit and drink my coffee and realize
that just like Otis Redding what I want is
"Security." But fool for wanton kisses
leaves me waiting out the morning.
Angry with the light.

Measure

In the traffic jam on the way to the picnic
I think of the Julio Cortázar short story.
Probably inspired by Godard's *Weekend* or maybe
he was trapped on the highway just outside
Paris for five hours of what was a 40-minute trip.
Minutes do not flash by or crawl, they tick.
Off toward destination—there is this little panic—
are we going in the right direction?

On the beach, I ask Dan and Nick how wide is Lake Tahoe.
Nick recoils from the question, looks at Dan and says:
"Why do women ask us these questions?
Don't they know we just make it up as we go along."
Dan nods, agreeing. He smiles.
"3.72 miles and the mountains are . . ."
"I know," I say. "It's all improvisation."

The scientists that Carrie McCray describes in her notes
for a poem on Otabenga come to mind.
How they measured his skull, digits, his penis
in search of what they desired: "The Missing Link."
Or Elizabeth Alexander's calculated retelling of the story of
    "The Venus
Hottentot," who was treated only as a curiosity
after the scientists realized she was human.
African.

Could it be that ease with ticking off the length of an ear,
the abacus's computation
the span of the measuring stick
the tape measure sprung, then recoiled
that makes women ask
how much
how many
how long

Connecting quantifiable time and distance is as dumbfounded
as the stars' lunatic mapmaking.
Or so it seemed the night I was drunk enough
to apprehend the shape of Orion's Belt.
I was blessed, puzzled.

Why can't I swing Orion's Belt around my waist
and dance that dance that starts and stops the cosmic traffic?
Why can't you?

We are stuck on this ground. In this traffic. On this beach.
Dry grasses bend beneath the weight of our feet.
And the hummingbird's flight stops conversation,
a mark in summer air.

Why these wet lawns full of grasses, insects, budding flowers
whose names we are to call?

We look across the lake. The mountains tremble
at an immeasurable speed.
And we have nothing to do with it.

What the God of Fire Charged Me

Pague lo que el dios de fuego/me cobró

—Ana Ilce

Each turn is the one that mocks
the old order and when the revolution happens
another readies itself.
Like the surge of blood in spring
or the lost hope of a winter
where kisses were too few or too many.

You will say,
"She's romantic."
And you will be correct.
But one dimension is only one dimension.
The others remain unseen.
Be wary.

When the night watch ends
and the sun rises—a smile on land and water—
I worry less about the dreams I cannot suppress
but more about the life
I am so willing to live.

One turn, then the other.
A fire walk as prelude.
A dance best forgiven.

New Blues

In bolder times, I'd be knee-deep in trouble:
kissing the brow of some dark-skinned dream of a man
or floating off the blasted brass in a smoky loft—draped in
silk-smooth cotton. But it's midnight in Dorchester, and
Robert Cray emphatically sings about wanting no more
of whatever was there before the song had to be sung.

It's a sad song. Funny, too. Hellhounds chased Robert Johnson
from one end of the Delta to the other.
But this singer's problem is much more local.
He just wants his lover to move out. Property is the new devil.
Who owns the lease gets to live. And sing about it.

Yes, the blues changes. Taught like economics or post-war
    poetry—
fussed over like a cranky aunt with money to leave behind.
Amusing and serious, this robust American tradition.
The blues and its borders.

In the movies, it gets very, very odd.
See *The Birth of the Blues,* in which Bing Crosby
and the boys create Dixieland jazz and take it from New
    Orleans
to Chicago.
Eddie "Rochester" Anderson is there to add a note of
    authenticity.
And Mary Martin is the "chick" singer.

The journey is drenched in glorious moonlight
in front of black and white
mattes designed by somebody German (probably).
As the boys (all white, mind you, except dear Rochester)
cheerfully play and fight,
"darkies" on the shore pick cotton, drink corn liquor, get
    lynched
and add to the exotic atmosphere.
A lone curl of smoke rises from a shack's

miserable chimney. Rochester wields his broom like a bayonet
as he escorts Miss Martin across the bridge between comic
    relief
and the lonesome, heartless voice of a blues man conjuring
    revenge.

After that, I ask, is there room for such cinematic loss in the
    New Blues?
Where are those hellhounds, those loose ends: women,
    whiskey bottle gone dry,
the sheriff from the next county coming to yours, that slap
    kick in the groin
after midnight and before the wolf's sad hour?

The pawnshops of memory are closed now. And some women
    refuse to slice
one more cheek over one last goodtime man. What to do?

When the last train whistle rasps, and only the jet's sonic boom
dazzles, will the drum kit slit the air and the saxophone

bend down so low
someone checks their back pockets as the guitar strips away
one more story: the one about the man and the woman,
the one about standing at the bridge,
the one told on the mockingbird's tongue
in a voice that scrapes the geologic layers of modern times
as if it could reveal the origins of the race.

But this morning, Cray's voice crawls off the phonograph,
a snake hungry for the future.
And I make one more cup of coffee, read critical theory,
then start to follow
the slithering line from ear to heart,
then back to the clock against the wall.

Halloween Weather (a Suite)

First Frost

In the booth across from me at Tom's Diner,
three Irish detectives talk about food and service.
They loudly denounce Brooklyn's lack of cuisine
and exult the glories of seafood in Myrtle Beach.

One guy says over and over
as he digs deeper into his banana walnut pancakes,
I could take it or leave it, but now
I just gotta have dessert.
Used to be 50/50,
but now I just gotta have it.

In the next block, the crack children
drift so fast they become wild clouds,
storm clouds swifter than the wind,

while up near the corner of Washington
and Sterling, their elders drink and drink
as the "oldies" station plays Smokey in his
twenties.

All week it's been Halloween weather,
still summer warm, but there's that hiss
from the North
chill.

Prayer

There are words that refuse me:
hermeneutics, tensile, circadian.

They feel like old expensive furniture
lovingly made for little use.

No, I should have learned them at eighteen
the way I learned to drink cheap wine.

No money again, just the usual dire straits
sharp dry leaves turn cyclone mean
and the full moon already gone.

Halloween weather, words of no use—
A mirror on the war within or just a popular song.

A tall poor Black man fiercely holds his elaborate CD player
as it outblasts all the obscenities on Vanderbilt Avenue.

And I know every one of them
by heart.

Down on my knees or down on my luck.
Lord, oh lord, deliver me.

Day of the Dead

Here is Brooklyn
here are the Anglos
here is the Day of the Dead

This makes sense, what with
all the blood spilled in battles
from Sheepshead Bay to Red Hook.
Not even a microscopic mention in the *Times*
unless five or more bats are used
to beat down the young men, mostly
Black, White, Hispanic
English-speaking?

So all these well-traveled people have brought back
perfect rituals appropriate really to the desert
and hills of Mexico. But we have our deserts,
our hills. Our bluffs and valleys too. Our bridges, our tunnels
and those subterranean maps like Escher's etchings—
rational schematics for daily trekking

from island to island
dream to dream.

So dressed in black from head to toe
we walk as if from one funeral to another
from Christian hymns to Buddhist sutras
always in this weather, a casual regard

for the walk from one street to the other
breathing the sugar-cube skeletons
happy for the privilege.

COLOPHON

This book was set in Spectrum and Rusticana Roman typefaces. It has been printed on acid-free paper and smyth sewn for durability and reading ease.